Keto Chaffle 2021

Recipes Cookbook

Discover delicious dishes with the complete fad in the ketogenic diet

By *Cris Chole*

TABLE of CONTENT

INTRODUCTION

An easy, safe way to lose weight and regulate blood sugar levels is the Ketogenic Diet. It has been proven that the Ketogenic Diet benefits those with elevated blood sugar content, type 2 diabetics (or pre-diabetes), PCOS (polycystic ovary syndrome) and even children with autism. However, for someone who wants a weight loss diet that does not leave you feeling hungry, it can also be perfect. It is, most importantly, a safe way to eat.

In order for any of this to work properly, you have to cut your carb intake using ketogenic carb recommendations. The main carb restriction states that your intake per meal should be no more than 13 grams of carbs. It also requires you go to embrace high-fat foods instead. Combine this with regular exercise and you can see the weight loss results you desire. To reduce carbohydrates in your diet, you'll need to remove or limit high-carb ingredients like all grains, lentils, legumes, potatoes, yams, yellow squash, sugars, honey, high-carb fruits, syrups, and the like. You can either avoid them or replace them with low-carb alternatives.

Whether you're looking to lose some weight or you need to burn fat, you can use the keto chaffle in your diet plan. Keto chaffle is a dietary supplement, with no calories or carbs. It contains low carbs and low calories as well. A keto chaffle is designed to help with weight loss.

How it works: the chaffle is made up of shredded coconut and pumpkin seeds. It works by providing a low-calorie carb source that provides energy to your body while keeping your blood sugar stable. As you continue using the chaffle, it helps to suppress hunger and increase fat burning.

The chaffle is made with coconut and pumpkin, making it a healthy low-carb alternative for anyone looking to lose weight. When used as part of a healthy diet, the chaffle helps stabilize blood sugar levels so the body has an easier time sensing when food is needed. The keto chaffle contains no calories or carbs, making it an ideal tool for anyone looking to lose or maintain their weight.

Regularly, keto dieters' lookout for ways to be accurate on the diet while searching for ways to make life easier at that. Chaffles are one of those foods that bring on a stimulating effect to the low-carb lifestyle. I find them to be an easy fix, and thankfully, they can be enjoyed different times of the day. In the recipes below, I share many ways to make and use chaffles —for breakfast through to dinner, snacks, and desserts.

This blend, therefore, makes dieting simpler as chaffles are enriched with healthy fats and mostly with no carbs. Reaching ketosis just got easier!

Finally, they are convenient for prep-ahead meals. And we know how prepping meals aids with effective keto dieting. Chaffles can be frozen for later use, and they taste excellent when warmed and enjoyed later.

Once you are hooked on chaffles, they will become a crucial part of your feeding because of the benefits that they bring. I have been making them continuously for weeks and thinking of creating a second cookbook of my new chaffle discoveries.

WHAT IS KETO DIET?

The word keto is short for ketogenic. The Ketogenic diet focuses on consuming very low amounts of carbohydrates, high levels of fat, and adequate levels of protein. In simple terms, with the Keto diet, you replace carbohydrates with fat. In case you haven't figured this out, carbohydrates are known as carbs, for short. You're probably wondering: The aim of a diet is to lose weight and not to gain more. How does that happen if I'm replacing carbs with fat? It is quite simple, really. When the levels of carbs in your body start to dwindle, your body goes into a metabolic state. This metabolic state is referred to as ketosis. The ketosis state is one in which the body burns fat much more rapidly to convert it into energy. The fat is not only turned to energy but is also turned into ketones. Ketones located in the liver also boost energy. In summary, Keto changes your body's mode of operation. Rather than converting your carbohydrates into energy, the fats you want to rid your body of are converted and burned off instead. The end result of a Keto diet is burned fat, boosted energy, reduced insulin levels, and reduced blood sugar.

Benefits of the Keto diet

The Keto diet has been proven to have many advantages for people over 50. Here are some of the best.

Eradicates inflammation

Few things are worse than the pain from an inflamed joint or muscle. Arthritis, for instance, can be extremely difficult to bear. When you follow the ketosis diet, the production of cytokines will be reduced. Cytokines cause inflammation and therefore, their eradication will reduce it.

It eradicates nutrients deficiency

Keto focuses on consuming exactly what you need. If you use a great Keto plan, your body will lack no nutrients and will not suffer any deficiency.

Reduced hunger

The reason we find it difficult to stick to diets is hunger. It doesn't matter your age; diets do not become easier. We may have a mental picture of the healthy body we want. We may even have clear visuals of the kind of life we want to lead once free from unhealthy living but none of that matters when hunger enters the scene. However, the Keto diet is a diet that combats this problem. The Keto diet focuses on consuming plenty of proteins. Proteins are filling and do not let you feel hungry too easily. In addition, when your carb levels are reduced, your appetite takes a hit. It is a win-win situation.

Weight loss

Keto not only burns fat, but it also reduces that craving for food. Combined, these are two great ways to lose weight. It is one of the diets that has proven to help the most when it comes to weight loss. The Keto diet has been proven to be one of the best ways to burn stubborn belly fat while keeping yourself revitalized and healthy.

Reduces blood sugar and insulin

After 50, monitoring blood sugar can be a real struggle. Cutting down on carbs drastically reduces both insulin levels and blood sugar levels. This means that the Keto diet will benefit millions as a lot of people struggle with insulin complications and high blood sugar levels. It has been proven to help as when some people embark on Keto, they cut up to half of the carbs they consume. It's a treasure for those with diabetes and insulin resistance. A study was carried out on people with type 2 diabetes. After cutting down on carbs, within six months, 95 percent of people were able to reduce or totally stop using their glucose-lowering medication.

Lower levels of triglycerides

A lot of people do not know what triglycerides are. Triglycerides are molecules of fat in your blood. They are known to circulate the bloodstream and can be very dangerous. High levels of triglycerides can cause heart failures and heart diseases. However, Keto is known to reduce these levels.

Reduces acne

Although acne is mostly suffered by those who are young, there are cases of people above 50 having it. Moreover, Keto is not only for persons after 50. Acne is not only caused by blocked pores. There are quite a number of things proven to cause it. One of these things is your blood sugar. When you consume processed and refined carbs, it affects gut bacteria and results in the fluctuation of blood sugar levels. When the gut bacteria and sugar levels are affected, the skin suffers. However, when you embark on the Keto diet, you cut off on carbs intake which means that in the very first place, your gut bacteria will not be affected thereby cutting off that avenue to develop.

Increases HDL levels

HDL refers to high-density lipoprotein. When your HDL levels are compared to your LDL levels and are not found low, your risk of developing a heart disease is lowered. This is great for persons over 50 as heart diseases suddenly become more probable. Eating fats and reducing your intake of carbohydrates is one of the most assured ways to increase your high-density lipoprotein levels.

Reduces LDL levels

High levels of LDL can be very problematic when you attain 50. This is because LDL refers to bad cholesterol. People with high levels of this cholesterol are more likely to get heart attacks. When you reduce the number of carbs you consume, you will increase the size of bad LDL particles. However, this will result in the reduction of the total LDL particles as they would have increased in size. Smaller LDL particles have been linked to heart diseases while larger ones have been proven to have lower risks attached.

May help combat cancer

I termed this under 'May' because research on this is not as extensive and conclusive as we would like it to be. However, there is proof supporting it. Firstly, it helps reduce the levels of blood sugar which in turn reduces insulin complications which in turn reduces the risk of developing cancers related to insulin levels. In addition, Keto places more oxidative stress on cancer cells than on normal cells thereby making it great for chemotherapy. The risk of developing cancer after fifty is still existent and so, Keto is literally a lifesaver.

May lower blood pressure

High blood pressure plagues adults much more than it does young ones. Once you attain 50, you must monitor your blood pressure rates. Reduction in the intake of carbohydrates is a proven way to lower your blood pressure. When you cut down on your carbs and lower your blood sugar levels, you greatly reduce your chances of getting some other diseases.

Combats metabolic syndrome

As you grow older, you may find that you struggle to control your blood sugar level. Metabolic syndrome is another condition that has been proven to have an influence on diabetes and heart disease development. The symptoms associated with metabolic syndrome include but are not limited to high triglycerides, obesity, high blood sugar level, and low levels of high-density lipoprotein cholesterol.

However, you will find that reducing your level of carbohydrate intake greatly affects this. You will improve your health and majorly attack all the above-listed symptoms. Keto diet helps to fight against metabolic syndrome which is a big win.

Great for the heart

People over the age of 50 have been proven to have more chances of developing heart diseases. Keto diet has been proven to be great for the heart. As it increases good cholesterol levels and reduces the levels of bad cholesterol, you will find that partaking in the Keto diet proves extremely beneficial for your health.

May reduce seizure risks

When you change your intake levels the combination of protein, fat, and carbs, as we explained before, your body will go into ketosis. Ketosis has been proven to reduce seizure levels in people who suffer from epilepsy. When they do not respond to treatment, the ketosis treatment is used. This has been done for decades.

Helps women suffering from polycystic ovarian syndrome (pros)

This syndrome affects women of all ages. PCOS is short for polycystic ovarian syndrome. Polycystic ovarian syndrome is an endocrine disorder that results in enlarged ovaries with cysts. These cysts are dangerous and cause other complications. It has been proven that a high intake of carbohydrates negatively affects women suffering from polycystic ovarian syndrome. When a woman with PCOS cuts down on carbs and embarks on the Keto diet, the polycystic ovarian syndrome falls under attack.

It is beyond doubt that the Keto diet is beneficial in so many ways that it almost looks unreal. If you are to embark on the Keto diet, there are several things you must know.

How to achieve ketosis

1. Withdraw carbohydrates from the diet. Most individuals have no difficulty limiting their consumption of carbohydrates to less than 100 grams of net carbohydrates per day. The total sum of carbohydrates minus the fiber is net carbs.
2. Increase fat in order to make up about 90% of your total caloric intake (in conjunction with step 1.)
3. Eat at least 50 grams of dietary fat a day for a meal, preferably for a single meal.
4. Consume at least one liter per day of water. Drink water at room temperature if you can, so that your insulin reaction won't spike. With your meals, don't drink water, as water will dilute your stomach's digestive enzymes, reducing their ability to break down and digest your food. Just before feeding, drink a glass or two of water to fill up your stomach and prime it for digestion.
5. Exercise in a state of fasting. Fasting exercise implies exercising on an empty stomach (or mostly empty stomach.)
6. To support weight loss, exercise frequently enough.

What is Chaffle

A chaffle, or cheese waffle, is an egg and cheese keto waffle. Chaffles become a popular snack of keto / low-carb. Easy Keto Chaffles Keto Chaffles seemed to pop into the low carb world overnight, and now they're here to stay. I'm sharing all the information I have in one place to make it easier to find. I tried a lot of different variants on this recipe, but I wanted to make sure that those looking for a keto-friendly bread low in carbs for the ketogenic diet would share the original recipe for the chaffle.

What is this keto Chaffle recipe in the world that has overtaken and conquered the keto community? Simply put, it's a cheese and egg waffle. There have been various variants in Facebook groups since the original recipe came out. It seems like every person in the world who practices the keto or low carb diet is making their Chaffles version.

WHAT DO YOU NEED TO PREPARE A CHAFFLE?

This list is not exhaustive, but this is a decent place to start. This consists of kettle, cooking utensils, and other devices for your kitchen productivity. Look at what you already have at home and make a list of the items you need to buy for your kitchen now. Much depends on the type of bite recipe you want to try.

Cast Iron Skillet: to have at least one is an absolute, bonus points if you have a few in different sizes. If you find a high-quality cast iron pan, you will get more value in the long run. In general, you will find that this cast iron pot will last for years. If you don't use a waffle maker, you definitely need a good pot or pan.

If you are a fan of a low-carbohydrate diet and especially the ketogenic diet, then you may have heard of Chaffles. And waffles are nothing more than waffles with very little carbohydrate, ketogenic and gluten-free, based on cheese. Therefore the name Chaffle = cheese + waffles.

This ketogenic waffle is perfect for breakfast with butter or berries and is used instead of bread with hamburgers, tomatoes and salads. The possibilities are endless!

Low-carb waffles are an alternative to the healthy, low-protein and low-sugar foods we all need for breakfast or after hard training. Usually, this is a rich oil and sugar that is clearly not suitable for a healthy and controlled diet. However, if you find the right dish, I can assure you that there is no low-carb waffle protein that envy traditional Belgian waffles. Soft and saturated textures along with low carbohydrate nutrients make this protein recipe mandatory, easy to prepare and adapt to your macro.

Exercising and keeping your body in shape is a difficult task and often involves the burden of not eating traditional and popular foods. We don't lack creativity and we are always ready to change traditional recipes with less fat and calories, but always good and delicious ingredients into healthier versions.

Waffles are a distinctive temptation in Northern Europe, crispy on the outside and soft on the inside. Very similar in texture and taste to pancakes, they differ in their distinctive honeycomb form, which means that they can absorb sweet sauce perfectly; from sweet to maple syrup to chocolate, hazelnuts or peanut cream.

Usually cooked with butter and sugar, I offer them today with a simple recipe that has nothing to offer besides the classic traditional Belgian waffles.

Baking basics

You'll need to have just a few pieces of equipment and learn some basic techniques before getting started in your baking practice.

BANNETON OR PROOFING BASKET: For the final proof, the dough needs to be placed in a basket that will allow air to circulate. You can buy baskets specifically for this called bannetons, which are made of cane. If you aren't ready to invest in a couple of bannetons just yet, a round or oval basket from a thrift store can be lined with a floured kitchen towel for a more affordable option. When I first started out, I had a ragtag collection of round and oval-shaped baskets, and they worked just fine.

BOWLS: I love using the large metal mixing bowl that I found at a restaurant supply store, but any bowl will do. Make sure you have a variety of sizes so you can measure out different quantities of ingredients. Whenever I shop at thrift stores, I like finding small bowls for a few cents here and there to add to my collection. Having little bowls for ingredients in smaller amounts, like salt, yeast, chopped herbs, and so on, is nice, but it's not absolutely necessary—any vessel will do.

CAST IRON DUTCH OVEN: This is needed for creating a high-heat, steam-enclosed environment to bake loaves in, and it's the best investment for baking artisan-style loaves in a home oven. You can find these on Amazon for about $35 or at your local kitchen store. Many people already have a cast iron or ceramic Dutch oven in their kitchen, but if you don't, it's well worth the investment. I use a Dutch oven in many of the recipes in the book.

DOUGH SCRAPER: I recommend getting a metal and a plastic dough scraper. They cost just a few dollars at kitchen stores, at restaurant supply stores, or on Amazon, and they are so useful. A metal scraper is helpful for cutting and scraping dough off your work area, and a plastic scraper is flexible enough to help scrape the dough out of the bowl after rising.

KITCHEN SCALE: Almost all of the ingredients in the recipes are measured in grams, so you will need a kitchen scale that weighs in metrics. Weighing your ingredients is the best way to get the most consistent results in your baking, and once you get used to weighing your ingredients, I promise you won't want to go back. It is so much simpler and makes a huge difference in the final loaf of bread. Kitchen scales are relatively inexpensive these days; small ones can be found for around $20. They typically have a "mode" button that will easily switch them from ounces to grams.

LOAF PANS: I recommend buying two 9-by-5-by-3-inch rectangular loaf pans, which is probably the most common size found at stores. My favorite pan is from USA Pan, and it can be found online. The loaves never ever stick to them. I use a 9-by-5-by-3-inch loaf pan for all of the loaf-style breads in this book.

NOTEBOOK AND PEN: I can't say enough that when you are starting out, different baking results will occur and you will want to know why you got those results. The only way to find out is to record what you did. Think of it like running a series of scientific experiments. Everything being equal, knowing what variables have changed and what haven't can lead you to where you went right or wrong.

PEEL: This is a flat wooden board with a handle for loading bread or pizza onto a baking stone in the oven. If you don't have one, it's no problem—I used a thin wooden cutting board for years, and it is a fine option.

PIZZA STONE OR BAKING STONE: These are preheated in the oven and help build the perfect crust while baking bread and pizza. If you don't have one, you can bake on an inverted baking sheet lined with parchment, but the results won't be quite the same.

RAZOR BLADE OR LAME: A razor blade is the best tool for slashing the top of a loaf of bread. A lame is a tool that holds the razor blade safely and has a nice handle, which makes it even easier to make precision slashes. My favorite lame is made by Mure & Peyrot and can be found on Amazon for only $15. You will as you move on to more advanced recipes.

RIMMED BAKING SHEET: This is an item you likely have in your kitchen already, and if not, it's a worthwhile investment. I usually use a 12-by-18-inch or a 16-by-24-inch baking sheet, which can be found at restaurant supply stores and online. In some recipes within this book, I call for a 16-by-24-inch baking sheet, but if a 12-by-18-inch sheet fits better in your oven, feel free to use that instead.

THERMOMETER: To achieve consistency in your baking, you'll need to know the temperature of your water and the ingredients. Buy a probe thermometer to check temperatures of ingredients. I also recommend you have an oven thermometer to be sure the temperature of your oven is accurate. You can purchase these for around $20 on Amazon and in most grocery stores.

Other items you may need that are usually part of any kitchen:
•Kitchen towels
•Nonstick cooking spray
•Parchment paper
•Pastry brush
•Plastic wrap
•Scissors
•Spray bottle
•Rubber spatula

KETO CHAFFLE BENEFITS

It also makes it easier to fast intermittently, something that can increase efforts to reverse type 2 diabetes and accelerate weight loss, beyond the effects of keto only. Plus, you might be able to do so. Most people feel just the need to feed on a keto diet twice a day (often skipping breakfast), and some just eat once a day. Not having to fight hunger symptoms could also potentially help with issues such as obesity or drug addiction. Eventually, feeling happy can be part of the solution, Food should avoid being an opponent and turn into your partner, or just food, whatever you like.

Low carb and diabetes reversal Control blood sugar to reverse type 2 diabetes Studies show that a ketogenic diet is ideal for the treatment of type 2 diabetes, even leading to complete reversal of the disease.

This makes perfect sense as keto decreases blood sugar levels, eliminates the need for medicine and reduces the potential negative effects of high levels of insulin.30 In the best case, long-term blood glucose can be so much changed that it returns to normal without treatment. In this context, reversal means progressing or getting worse the opposite of the disease. Lifestyle changes, though, only work when you do it. If a person returns to the lifestyle that he or she had when diabetes type 2 emerged and advanced, it is possible that they will recover and improve again over time.

How to reverse type 2 diabetes 200 + success stories Low carb and diabetes reversal Improved health markers many studies show that low-carb diets improve several major risk factors for heart disease, including the cholesterol profile, which includes cholesterol and triglycerides of high-density lipoprotein (HDL).

How To Maximize Stamina On a Keto Diet

Keto diet and epilepsy: Epilepsy the Ketogenic diet is a proven and often effective epilepsy medical therapy used since the 1920s. It has historically been used mainly for infants, but it has also helped adults in recent years. Using a Ketogenic diet for epilepsy will allow some people to take less or none anti-epileptic medications while being potentially seizure-free. This can reduce side effects of drugs and increase mental performance as a result.

How To Live Healthy From Low Carb

A low-carb diet is poor in carbs, found mainly in sugar, pasta and bread. Then, you eat foods that include plant proteins, fats and vegetables. Studies show that low-carb diets lead to weight loss and improved markers of health. For decades, these diets have been widely used and are recommended by many physicians. Best of all, calories do not usually need to be counted or special products used. All you need to do is eat whole foods that make a diet that is complete, nutritious and filling. A low-carb diet means you're eating less carbohydrates and more fat. A low-carb, high-fat diet (LCHF) or a keto diet can also be called.

They have been advised for decades that fat is detrimental to our health. In the meantime low-fat "diet" products have flooded supermarket shelves, often full of sugar. This was probably a major misunderstanding, which coincided with the onset of the epidemic of obesity. Although this does not prove causation, it is clear that the low-fat campaign did not prevent an increase in obesity, and it may have led to it. Studies now show no reason to be afraid of natural fats. Instead, your friend is on a low-carb diet. Just minimize your sugar and starch intake and you can eat all the fat you need to be satisfied with. If you avoid sugar and starch, your blood sugar tends to stabilize and the fat-storing hormone levels drop in insulin. This helps increase the burning of fat and makes you feel satiated, naturally reducing the intake of food and promoting weight loss. Studies show that a low-carb diet can make weight loss simpler and, among other advantages, regulate the blood sugar.

Who is not expected to have a strict low-carb diet?

Some people can safely initiate a low-carb diet.13 But you may need some planning or modification in these three situations: are you taking diabetes medication, such as insulin, for example? Learn more Do you take high blood pressure medication? Discover more Are you breastfeeding at the moment? Learn more If you're not in any of these groups and you don't have any other severe chronic conditions, you're good to go!

Why do I have to try low-carb diet?

The issue with carbohydrates is that we tend to consume more than is actually needed for our bodies. For this reason, carbohydrates not burned off as energy are converted into sugars and stored in the body as fat. This is why after the initial burst of energy from a meal filled with carbohydrates, you can feel sluggish.

A low-carb diet does not require you to completely cut carbohydrates out of your life. Instead, it tells you to limit the number of carbohydrates you eat to what you currently burn from physical activity, and to remember where the carbs you consume come from.

What am I allowed to eat?

The issue that many people have with living low-carb is that they feel they have limited food options, but it doesn't have to be that way. In addition to plenty of delicious vegetables, a healthy low carb diet will include meat, fish, and eggs. A low-carb diet doesn't have to get repetitive as nuts and berries as well as some healthy fats can be included. As a result, many people living on low-carb diets consider that their diets are much more complex, flexible, and fascinating than before a low-carb diet is implemented. For those who want to lose weight, a low carb diet may be worth an attempt and are willing to cut down on carbs to do so. A low-carb diet can be healthy, nutritious, and tasty if you choose lean proteins as well as some fruits and vegetables, and even some fats and whole grains to make it a diet that you can consume and enjoy.

How To Boost Metabolism From Low Carb

The basic low-calorie diets do not work well when it comes to permanent weight loss. While it is true that in order to lose weight, you need to be in a calorie deficit, simple calorie counting is not a useful strategy for sustained weight loss.

Your metabolism is caused by a lot of weight loss. In a nutshell, your appetite is how much energy you use all day long, and how well the body is using that energy.

You have a great deal of control over how your metabolism works. Improving your metabolism makes weight loss faster, and maintaining your metabolism is a good predictor of a long, healthy life.

What does metabolism mean?

Your metabolism is the collection of daily energy-creating processes your body uses. Your metabolism fuels all you do, so becoming friendly with it is worthwhile. Which includes finding out how your metabolism can be assisted and rendered as high as possible?

The three main roles of your metabolism are:

Converting food into energy for your cells

Converting food into building blocks for proteins and fats to maintain the tissues of your body.

Eliminating waste from your body. It produces energy, breaks down and rebuilds cells and bone, and removes waste, making it impossible to accurately measure the actual daily metabolism.

Nonetheless, calories — a measure of the heat generated during combustion— are one way of measuring the food's energy content and determining how much food the body needs every day.

Calorie needs change from day to day, and the two terms are not synonymous because your daily calorie needs are linked to your metabolism. Metabolism is more than just the calories you're eating.

How Your Body Burns Food: Based on the presence or absence of oxygen, your body also has two forms of food-burning.

Anaerobic metabolism that occurs during intensive exercise or when your body is deprived of oxygen depends on glucose (simple sugar), lactate (burning sugar by-product) and fuel amino acids (protein). Anaerobically, you can't burn fat.

What Does Good Metabolism Contribute

There are a wide range of factors that influence the metabolism.

#1: Less lean muscle mass: The faster your metabolism will be, the leaner muscle mass you get. Muscle uses more energy than fat, which means it will increase the basal metabolic rate by adding on muscle, and the more athletic you are, the more calories you will eat in a day.

#2: Running speeds up your metabolism, during and after the running.

#3: Hormone levels: Often contribute to your particular metabolic profile is your hormone levels. Energy regulating hormones such as cortisol, thyroid hormones, and insulin can interact with each other to accelerate or slow your metabolism. Diet, sleep, stress and other factors in the lifestyle play a major role in the function of your hormone.

#4: Diet: Diet directly affects your metabolic rate, through the thermal effect of food, and indirectly through your hormones and the flora of your gut.

#5: Age: Eventually, the metabolism is affected by age. Your metabolism slows down as you get older.

Healthy, well-metabolized people usually have relatively high lean muscle mass, are physically active, have balanced hormones, and are healthier and balanced than the gut bacteria of overweight people has intestinal bacteria.

How hunger mode affects your metabolism hunger mode is a term for the natural response of your body to a permanent, extreme caloric shortage.

The transition can also lead to the following as your muscles, central nervous system, and hormones work together to suppress your appetite and regulate your body weight: exhaustion Physical inactivity Excessive food cravings Food cravings Long-term hunger behavior can lead to severe hormonal imbalances, extreme difficulties sustaining healthy body weight, and health problems. These harmful effects are referred to as "metabolic damage." Metabolic damage includes appetite hormone destruction, loss of lean muscle mass, and, in severe cases, organ damage. Researchers have recorded hair loss, asthma, and heart failure from long-term, very-low-calorie diets due to metabolic harm. To be clear, the mode of starvation is not the same as a calorie deficit that is mild or short term. Starvation mode exists when you under eat regularly and the body doesn't even get close to the energy it needs. If you're going to lose weight, it's imperative that you prepare well to escape starvation mode and minimize metabolic damage.

BREAKFAST

Peanut Butter and Jelly Sammich Chaffle

Preparation Time: 20 minutes
Cooking Time: 30 minutes
Servings: 2

Ingredients:
For Chaffle:

- Egg: 2
- Mozzarella: 1/4 cup
- Vanilla extract: 1 tbsp.
- Coconut flour: 2 tbsp.
- Baking powder: 1/4 tsp.
- Cinnamon powder: 1 tsp.
- Swerve sweetener: 1 tbsp.
- For Blueberry Compote:
- Blueberries: 1 cup
- Lemon zest: 1/2 tsp.
- Lemon juice: 1 tsp.
- Xanthan gum: 1/8 tsp.
- Water: 2 tbsp.
- Swerve sweetener: 1 tbsp.

Directions:
1. For the blueberry compote, add all the ingredients except xanthan gum to a small pan
2. Mix them all and boil
3. Set the heat and simmer for 8-10 minutes; the sauce will initiate to thicken
4. Add xanthan gum now and stir
5. Now remove the pan from the stove and allow the mixture to cool down
6. Put in refrigerator
7. Preheat a mini waffle maker if needed and grease it
8. In a mixing bowl, add all the chaffle ingredients and mix well
9. Pour the mixture to the lower plate of the waffle maker and spread it evenly to cover the plate properly
10. Close the lid
11. Cooking for at least 4 minutes to get the desired crunch
12. Remove the chaffle from the heat and keep aside
13. Make as many chaffles as your mixture and waffle maker allow
14. Serve with the blueberry and enjoy!

Nutrition: Calories: 175 Total Fat: 15g Carbs: 8g Net Carbs: 5g Fiber: 3g Protein: 6g

Peanut Butter Cup Chaffles

Preparation Time: 5 minutes
Cooking Time: 15 minutes
Servings: 1

Ingredients:
For the chaffle:
- Eggs: 1
- Mozzarella cheese: 1/2 cup shredded
- Cocoa powder: 2 tbsp.
- Espresso powder: 1/4 tsp.
- Sugar free chocolate chips: 1 tbsp.

For the filling:
- Peanut butter: 3 tbsp.
- Butter: 1 tbsp.
- Powdered sweetener: 2 tbsp.

Direction:
1. Add all the chaffle ingredients in a bowl and whisk
2. Preheat your mini waffle iron if needed and grease it
3. Cooking your mixture in the mini waffle iron for at least 4 minutes
4. Make two chaffles
5. Mix the filling ingredients together.
6. When chaffles cool down, spread peanut butter on them to make a sandwich

Nutrition: Calories: 448 Total Fat: 34g Carbs: 17g Net Carbs: 10g Fiber: 7g Protein: 24g

Chocolaty Chaffles

Preparation Time: 5 minutes
Cooking Time: 15 minutes
Servings: 1

Ingredients:

- Eggs: 1
- Mozzarella cheese: 1/2 cup shredded
- Cocoa powder: 2 tbsp.
- Espresso powder: 1/4 tsp.
- Sugar free chocolate chips: 1 tbsp.

Directions:

1. Add all the chaffle ingredients in a bowl and whisk
2. Preheat your mini waffle iron if needed and grease it
3. Cooking your mixture in the mini waffle iron for at least 4 minutes
4. Make as many chaffles as you can

Nutrition: Calories: 258 Total Fat: 23g Carbs: 12g Net Carbs: 6g Fiber: 6g Protein: 5g

Mc Griddle Chaffle

Preparation Time: 5 minutes
Cooking Time: 10 minutes
Servings: 2

Ingredients:
- Egg: 2
- Mozzarella cheese: 11/2 cup (shredded)
- Maple Syrup: 2 tbsp. (sugar-free)
- Sausage patty: 2
- American cheese: 2 slices
- Swerve/Monkfruit: 2 tbsp.

Directions:
1. Preheat a mini waffle maker if needed and grease it
2. In a mixing bowl, beat eggs and add shredded Mozzarella cheese, Swerve/Monkfruit, and maple syrup
3. Merge them all well and pour the mixture to the lower plate of the waffle maker
4. Close the lid
5. Cooking for at least 4 minutes to get the desired crunch
6. Remove the chaffle from the heat
7. sausage patty by following the instruction given on the packaging
8. Place a cheese slice on the patty immediately when removing from heat
9. Take two chaffles and put sausage patty and cheese in between
10. Make as many chaffles as your mixture and waffle maker allow
11. Serve hot and enjoy!

Nutrition: Calories: 231 Total Fat: 20g Carbs: 8g Net Carbs: 6g Fiber: 2g Protein: 9g

Cinnamon Swirl Chaffles

Preparation Time: 5 minutes
Cooking Time: 10 minutes
Servings: 2

Ingredients:
For Chaffle:

- Egg: 2
- Cream Cheese: 2 oz. softened
- Almond flour: 2 tbsp.
- Vanilla Extract: 2 tsp.
- Cinnamon: 2 tsp.
- Vanilla extract: 2 tsp.
- Splenda: 2 tbsp.

For Icing:

- Cream cheese: 2 oz. softened
- Splenda: 2 tbsp.
- Vanilla: 1 tsp.
- Butter: 2 tbsp. unsalted butter

For Cinnamon Drizzle:

- Splenda: 2 tbsp.
- Butter: 1 tbsp.
- Cinnamon: 2 tsp.

Directions:
1. Preheat the waffle maker
2. Grease it lightly
3. Mix all the chaffle ingredients together
4. Pour the mixture to the waffle maker
5. Cooking for around 4 minutes or till chaffles become crispy
6. Keep them aside when done
7. In a small bowl, mix the ingredients of icing and cinnamon drizzle
8. Heat it in a microwave for about 10 seconds to gain a soft uniformity
9. Whirl on cooled chaffles and enjoy!

Nutrition: Calories: 323 Total Fat: 27g Carbs: 8g Net Carbs: 3g; Fiber: 5g Protein: 15g

Raspberries Chaffle

Preparation time: 15 minutes
Cooking Time: 15 Minutes
Servings: 1

Ingredients:
- 1 egg white
- 1/4 cup jack cheese, shredded
- 1/4 cup cheddar cheese, shredded
- 1 tsp. coconut flour
- 1/4 tsp. baking powder
- 1/2 tsp. stevia

For Topping
- 4 oz. raspberries
- 2 tbsps. coconut flour
- 2 oz. unsweetened raspberry sauce

Directions:
1. Switch on your round Waffle Maker and grease it with cooking spray once it is hot.
2. Mix together all chaffle ingredients in a bowl and combine with a fork.
3. Pour chaffle batter in a preheated maker and close the lid.
4. Roll the taco chaffle around using a kitchen roller, set it aside and allow it to set for a few minutes.
5. Once the taco chaffle is set, remove from the roller.
6. Dip raspberries in sauce and arrange on taco chaffle.
7. Drizzle coconut flour on top.
8. Enjoy raspberries taco chaffle with keto coffee.

Nutrition: Calories: 386 Total Fat: 37g Carbs: 13g Net Carbs: 8g; Fiber: 5g Protein: 5g

Garlic and Parsley Chaffles

Preparation time: 10 minutes
Cooking Time: 5 Minutes
Servings: 1

Ingredients:
- 1 large egg
- 1/4 cup cheese Mozzarella
- 1 tsp. coconut flour
- 1/4 tsp. baking powder
- 1/2 tsp. garlic powder
- 1 tbsp. minute sced parsley

For Serving
- 1 Poach egg
- 4 oz. smoked salmon

Directions:
1. Switch on your Dash waffle maker and let it preheat.
2. Grease waffle maker with cooking spray.
3. Mix together egg, mozzarella, coconut flour, and baking powder, and garlic powder, parsley to a mixing bowl until combined well.
4. Pour batter in circle chaffle maker.
5. Close the lid.
6. Cooking for about 2-3 minutes or until the Chaffles is Cooked.
7. Serve with smoked salmon and poached egg.
8. Enjoy!

Nutrition: Calories: 757 Total Fat: 38g Carbs: 17g Net Carbs: 11g Fiber: 6g Protein: 29g

Scrambled Eggs and a Spring Onion Chaffle

Preparation time: 10 minutes
Cooking Time: 7-9 Minutes
Servings: 4

Ingredients:

Batter

- 4 eggs
- 2 cups grated Mozzarella cheese
- 2 spring onions, finely chopped
- Salt and pepper to taste
- 1/2 teaspoon dried garlic powder
- 2 tablespoons almond flour
- 2 tablespoons coconut flour

Other

- 2 tablespoons butter for brushing the waffle maker
- 6-8 eggs
- Salt and pepper
- 1 teaspoon Italian spice mix
- 1 tablespoon olive oil
- 1 tablespoon freshly chopped parsley

Directions:
1. Preheat the waffle maker.
2. Whisk the eggs into a bowl and add the grated cheese.
3. Mix until just combined, then add the chopped spring onions and season with salt and pepper and dried garlic powder.
4. Stir in the almond flour and mix until everything is combined.
5. Brush the heated waffle maker with butter and add a few tablespoons of the batter.
6. Close the lid and Cooking for about 7–8 minutes depending on your waffle maker.
7. While the chaffles are Cooking, the scrambled eggs by whisking the eggs in a bowl until frothy, about 2 minutes. Flavor with salt and black pepper to taste and add the Italian spice mix. Whisk to blend in the spices.
8. Warm the oil in a non-stick pan over medium heat.
9. Pour the eggs in the pan and Cooking until eggs are set to your liking.
10. Serve each chaffle and top with some scrambled eggs. Top with freshly chopped parsley.

Nutrition: Calories: 165 Total Fat: 15 Carbs: 4g Net Carbs: 2g Fiber: 2g Protein: 6g

Egg and Cheddar Cheese Chaffle

Preparation time: 10 minutes
Cooking Time: 7-9 Minutes
Servings: 4

Ingredients:

Batter
- 4 eggs
- 2 cups shredded white cheddar cheese
- Salt and pepper to taste

Other
- 2 tablespoons butter for brushing the waffle maker
- 4 large eggs
- 2 tablespoons olive oil

Directions:
1. Preheat the waffle maker.
2. Beat the eggs into a bowl and whisk them with a fork.
3. Stir in the grated cheddar cheese and season with salt and pepper.
4. Brush the heated waffle maker with butter and add a few tablespoons of the batter.
5. Close the lid and Cooking for about 7–8 minutes depending on your waffle maker.
6. While chaffles are Cooking, Cooking the eggs.
7. Set the oil in a large non-stick pan that has a lid over medium-low heat for 2-3 minutes
8. Crack an egg in a small ramekin and gently add it to the pan. Repeat the same way for the other 3 eggs.
9. Cover and let Cooking for 2 to 2 1/2 minutes for set eggs but with runny yolks.
10. Remove from heat.
11. To serve, place a chaffle on each plate and top with an egg. Flavor with salt and black pepper to taste.

Nutrition: Calories: 74 Total Fat: 7g Carbs: 1g Net Carbs: 0g Fiber: 0g Protein: 3g

Chili Chaffle

Preparation time: 10 minutes
Cooking Time: 7-9 Minutes
Servings: 4

Ingredients:

Batter
- 4 eggs
- 1/2 cup grated parmesan cheese
- 11/2 cups grated yellow cheddar cheese
- 1 hot red chili pepper
- Salt and pepper to taste
- 1/2 teaspoon dried garlic powder
- 1 teaspoon dried basil
- 2 tablespoons almond flour

Other
- 2 tablespoons olive oil for brushing the waffle maker

Directions:
1. Preheat the waffle maker.
2. Whisk the eggs into a bowl and add the grated parmesan and cheddar cheese.
3. Mix until just combined and add the chopped chili pepper. Season with salt and pepper, dried garlic powder and dried basil. Stir in the almond flour.
4. Mix until everything is combined.
5. Brush the heated waffle maker with olive oil and add a few tablespoons of the batter.
6. Close the lid and Cooking for about 7–8 minutes depending on your waffle maker.

Nutrition: Calories: 859 Total Fat: 73g Carbs: 8g Net Carbs: 8g Fiber: 0g Protein: 41g

LUNCH

Crunchy Fish and Chaffle Bites

Preparation Time: 10 minutes
Cooking Time: 15 minutes
Servings: 2

Ingredients:
- 1 lb. cod fillets, sliced into 4 slices
- 1 tsp. sea salt
- 1 tsp. garlic powder
- 1 egg, whisked
- 1 cup almond flour
- 2 tbsp. avocado oil

Chaffle Ingredients:
- 2 eggs
- 1/2 cup cheddar cheese
- 2 tbsp. almond flour
- 1/2 tsp. Italian seasoning

Directions:
1. Mix together chaffle ingredients in a bowl and make 4 squares.
2. Put the chaffles in a preheated chaffle maker.
3. Mix together the salt, pepper, and garlic powder in a mixing bowl. Toss the cod cubes in this mixture and let sit for 10 minutes.
4. Then dip each cod slice into the egg mixture and then into the almond flour.
5. Heat oil in skillet and fish cubes for about 2-3 minutes, until cooked and browned.
6. Serve on chaffles and enjoy!

Nutrition: Protein: 38 Fat: 59 Carbohydrates: 11

Grill Pork Chaffle Sandwich

Preparation Time: 10 minutes
Cooking Time: 15 minutes
Servings: 2

Ingredients:
- 1/2 cup mozzarella, shredded
- 1 egg
- I pinch garlic powder
- Pork Patty:
- 1/2 cup pork, minutes
- 1 tbsp. green onion, diced
- 1/2 tsp. Italian seasoning
- Lettuce leaves

Directions:
1. Preheat the square waffle maker and grease it.
2. Mix together egg, cheese and garlic powder in a small mixing bowl.
3. Pour batter in a preheated waffle maker and close the lid.
4. Make 2 chaffles from this batter.
5. Cooking chaffles for about 2-3 minutes until cooked through.
6. Meanwhile, mix together pork patty ingredients in a bowl and make 1 large patty.
7. Grill pork patty in a preheated grill for about 3-4 minutes per side until cooked through.
8. Arrange pork patty between two chaffles with lettuce leaves. Cut sandwich to make a triangular sandwich.
9. Enjoy!

Nutrition: Protein: 48 Fat: 48 Carbohydrates: 4

Chaffle and Chicken Lunch Plate

Preparation Time: 10 minutes
Cooking Time: 15 minutes
Servings: 2

Ingredients:
- 1 large egg
- 1/2 cup jack cheese, shredded
- 1 pinch salt

For Serving:
- 1 chicken leg
- Salt
- Pepper
- 1 tsp. garlic
- 1 egg
- 1 tsp. avocado oil

Directions:
1. Heat your square waffle maker and grease with Cooking spray.
2. Pour Chaffle batter into the skillet and Cooking for about 3 minutes.
3. Meanwhile, heat oil in a pan, over medium heat.
4. Once the oil is hot, add chicken thigh and garlic then, Cooking for about 5 minutes. Flip and Cooking for another 3-4 minutes.
5. Season with salt and pepper and give them a good mix.
6. Transfer cooked thigh to plate.
7. Set the egg in the same pan for about 1-2 minutes according to your choice.
8. Once chaffles are cooked, serve with fried egg and chicken thigh.
9. Enjoy!

Nutrition: Protein: 31 Fat: 66 Carbohydrates: 2

Chaffle Minutes Sandwich

Preparation Time: 10 minutes
Cooking Time: 10 minutes
Servings: 2

Ingredients:
- 1 large egg
- 1/8 cup almond flour
- 1/2 tsp. garlic powder
- 3/4 tsp. baking powder
- 1/2 cup shredded cheese

Sandwich Filling:
- 2 slices deli ham
- 2 slices tomatoes
- 1 slice cheddar cheese

Directions:
1. Grease your square waffle maker and preheat it on medium heat.
2. Mix together chaffle ingredients in a mixing bowl until well combined.
3. Pour batter into a square waffle and make two chaffles.
4. Once chaffles are cooked, remove from the maker.
5. For a sandwich, arrange deli ham, tomato slice and cheddar cheese between two chaffles.
6. Cut sandwich from the center.
7. Serve and enjoy!

Nutrition: Protein: 29 Fat: 66 Carbohydrates: 4

Chicken Zinger Chaffle

Preparation Time: 10 minutes
Cooking Time: 15 minutes
Servings: 2

Ingredients:

- 1 chicken breast, cut into 2 pieces
- 1/2 cup coconut flour
- 1/4 cup finely grated Parmesan
- 1 tsp. paprika
- 1/2 tsp. garlic powder
- 1/2 tsp. onion powder
- 1 tsp. salt and pepper
- 1 egg beaten
- Avocado oil for frying
- Lettuce leaves
- BBQ sauce

Chaffle Ingredients:

- 4 oz. cheese
- 2 whole eggs
- 2 oz. almond flour
- 1/4 cup almond flour
- 1 tsp. baking powder

Directions:

1. Mix together chaffle ingredients in a bowl.
2. Pour the chaffle batter in preheated greased square chaffle maker.
3. Cooking chaffles for about 2 minutes until cooked through.
4. Make square chaffles from this batter.
5. Meanwhile mix together coconut flour, parmesan, paprika, garlic powder, onion powder salt and pepper in a bowl.
6. Dip chicken first in coconut flour mixture then in beaten egg.
7. Heat avocado oil in a skillet and Cooking chicken from both sides, until lightly brown and cooked.
8. Set chicken zinger between two chaffles with lettuce and BBQ sauce.
9. Enjoy!

Nutrition: Protein: 30 Fat: 60 Carbohydrates: 9

Double Chicken Chaffles

Preparation Time: 10 minutes
Cooking Time: 5 minutes
Servings: 2

Ingredients:

- 1/2 cup boil shredded chicken
- 1/4 cup cheddar cheese
- 1/8 cup parmesan cheese
- 1 egg
- 1 tsp. Italian seasoning
- 1/8 tsp. garlic powder
- 1 tsp. cream cheese

Directions:

1. Preheat the Belgian waffle maker.
2. Mix together in chaffle ingredients in a bowl and mix together.
3. Sprinkle 1 tbsp. of cheese in a waffle maker and pour in chaffle batter.
4. Pour 1 tbsp. of cheese over batter and close the lid.
5. Cooking chaffles for about 4 to minutes.
6. Serve with a chicken zinger and enjoy the double chicken flavor.

Nutrition: Protein: 30 Fat: 65 Carbohydrates: 5

Chaffles with Zucchini Topping

Preparation Time: 10 minutes
Cooking Time: 10 minutes
Servings: 2

Ingredients:
- 1 large egg
- 1 tbsp. almond flour
- 1 tbsp. full-fat Greek yogurt
- 1/8 tsp. baking powder
- 1/4 cup shredded Swiss cheese

Topping:
- 4oz. grill prawns
- 4 oz. steamed cauliflower mash
- 1/2 zucchini sliced
- 3 lettuce leaves
- 1 tomato, sliced
- 1 tbsp. flax seeds

Directions:
1. Make 3 chaffles with the given chaffles ingredients.
2. For serving, arrange lettuce leaves on each chaffle.
3. Top with zucchini slice, grill prawns, cauliflower mash and a tomato slice.
4. Drizzle flax seeds on top.
5. Serve and enjoy!

Nutrition: Protein: 45 Fat: 47 Carbohydrates: 8

Chaffle with Melted Cheese and Bacon

Preparation Time: 10 minutes
Cooking Time: 15 minutes
Servings: 2

Ingredients:
- 1 egg
- 1/2 cup cheddar cheese, shredded
- 1 tbsp. parmesan cheese
- 3/4 tsp. coconut flour
- 1/4 tsp. baking powder
- 1/8 tsp. Italian Seasoning
- Pinch of salt
- 1/4 tsp. garlic powder

For Topping:
- 1 bacon sliced, Cooked and chopped
- 1/2 cup mozzarella cheese, shredded
- 1/4 tsp. parsley, chopped

Directions:
1. Preheat oven to 400 degrees.
2. Switch on your Mini Waffle Maker and grease with Cooking spray.
3. Mix together chaffle ingredients in a mixing bowl until combined.
4. Spoon half of the batter in the center of the waffle maker and close the lid. Cooking chaffles for about 3 minutes until cooked.
5. Carefully remove chaffles from the maker.
6. Arrange chaffles in a greased baking tray.
7. Top with mozzarella cheese, chopped bacon and parsley.
8. And bake in the oven for 4-5 minutes.
9. Once the cheese is melted, remove from the oven.
10. Serve and enjoy!

Nutrition: Protein: 28 Fat: 69 Carbohydrates: 3

Breakfast Cauliflower Chaffles and Tomatoes

Preparation Time: 10 minutes
Cooking Time: 15 minutes
Servings: 2

Ingredients:
- 1/2 cup cauliflower
- 1/4 tsp. garlic powder
- 1/4 tsp. black pepper
- 1/4 tsp. Salt
- 1/2 cup shredded cheddar cheese
- 1 egg

For Topping:
- 1 lettuce leave
- 1 tomato sliced
- 4 oz. cauliflower steamed, mashed
- 1 tsp. sesame seeds

Directions:
1. Add all chaffle ingredients into a blender and mix well.
2. Sprinkle 1/8 shredded cheese on the waffle maker and pour cauliflower mixture in a preheated waffle maker and sprinkle the rest of the cheese over it.
3. Cooking chaffles for about 4-5 minutes until cooked.
4. For serving, lay lettuce leaves over chaffle top with steamed cauliflower and tomato.
5. Drizzle sesame seeds on top.
6. Enjoy!

Nutrition: Protein: 25 Fat: 65 Carbohydrates: 10

DINNER

Pumpkin Chaffle with Cream Cheese Frosting

Preparation Time: 3 minutes
Cooking Time: 8 minutes
Servings: 2

Ingredients:
- 1 egg
- 1/2 cup of mozzarella cheese
- 1/2 tsp. pumpkin pie spice
- 1 tbs. pumpkin solid packed with no sugar added
- Optional Cream Cheese Frosting Ingredients:
- 2 tbs. softened and room temperature cream cheese
- 2 tbs. any of your favorite keto-friendly sweetener
- 1/2 tsp. clear extract of vanilla

Directions:
1. Heat the mini waffle maker.
2. Whip the egg in a little bowl.
3. Mix the cheese, pumpkin pie spice, and pumpkin in a mixing bowl.
4. Mix well.
5. Cooking for at least 3 to 4 minutes, until golden brown, in the mini waffle maker with half of the mixture.
6. When the chaffle is baking, mix all of the ingredients for the cream cheese frosting in a mixing bowl and whisk until smooth and fluffy.
7. Serve the hot chaffle with the cream cheese frosting right away.

Nutrition: Calories: 266 Carbohydrates: 2g Fat: 23g Protein: 13g

Chaffle Bread Pudding With Cranberries

Preparation Time: 10 minutes
Cooking Time: 30 minutes
Servings: 2

Ingredients:

Chaffles:

- 4 eggs
- 1 cup of shredded part skim mozzarella - cheese

Pudding:

- 3 beaten eggs
- 2 tsp. extract of vanilla
- 2 tsp. pumpkin pie spice
- 1/4 cup of So Nourished Erythritol sweetener blend
- 1/2 cup of canned pumpkin
- 1/2 cup of heavy cream
- 1/2 cup of fresh or frozen cranberries
- 1 tbsp. granulated Erythritol to sprinkle on top

Directions:

Chaffles:
1. Heat the waffle maker
2. In a mixing bowl, merge together the eggs and grated cheese.
3. Cooking chaffles in a waffle maker; depending on the unit, you'll get 4-6 chaffles/waffles.
4. Cooking 1/4 cup of batter at a time in a mini waffle machine (3-4 minutes every)
5. You can cook all of the batter at once in a full-size waffle maker for around 7 minutes.
6. Allow chaffles to cool on a rack before serving.

Bread Pudding:
1. Heat the oven to 350F. Tear the chaffles into bite-size bits with your hands.
2. Mix beaten eggs, milk, pumpkin, vanilla, spice blend, and sweetener in a mixing bowl.
3. To mix, whisk all together thoroughly.
4. Pour onto a pie plate that has been greased.
5. Top with cranberries and a little sugar if needed (if desired)
6. Heat oven to 350F and bake for 30 minutes, or until set.
7. Serve warm or cold with ice cream on top (if desired)

Nutrition: Calories: 160 Total Fat: 12g Cholesterol: 24mg Sodium: 93mg Carbohydrates: 4g Fiber: 1g Sugar: 1g Protein: 9g

Pumpkin Chaffles

Preparation Time: 5 minutes
Cooking Time: 8 minutes
Servings: 2

Ingredients:

- 1 oz. softened cream cheese
- 1 large egg
- 1 tbsp. pumpkin puree
- 1/2 tsp. pumpkin spice
- 1 tbsp. superfine almond flour
- 1/4 tsp. baking powder
- 1/2 tsp. Erythritol granular

Directions:

1. In a bowl, stir cream cheese until it reveres a whipped consistency. If the cream cheese is too hard to whisk, melt it in the microwave for a few seconds at a time (no more than 5 seconds at a time). If you Cooking the cream cheese for too long, it will overheat and splatter all over your oven.
2. In another bowl, merge together the egg and pumpkin puree until creamy. Whisk in the pumpkin spice and almond flour until well mixed. Whether you're using baking powder and sweetener, mix them together so they're equally distributed.
3. Waffle iron should be preheated. Grease the waffle iron with Cooking oil spray when it's ready.
4. Half of the batter can be poured into the mini waffle maker. Your batter should fill in all of the gaps. Waffle iron should be closed. Allow for 4-5 minutes of Cooking time, or until the waffle is dark brown and crispy on the outside. Continue for the remaining hitter. Using the Dash mini waffle machine, you should have enough batter to produce two chaffles.

Nutrition: Calories: 116.26 Carbohydrates: 2.61g Protein: 4.52g Fat: 9.54g Cholesterol: 121.1mg Potassium: 131.34mg,

Keto Pumpkin Cheesecake Chaffle

Preparation Time: 2 minutes
Cooking Time: 4 minutes
Servings: 2

Ingredients:

Pumpkin Chaffle:
- 1 Egg
- 1/2 cup of Mozzarella Cheese
- 1 1/2 tbsp. Pumpkin Puree
- 1 tbsp. Almond Flour
- 1 tbsp. of your choice sweetener
- 2 tsp. Heavy Cream
- 1 tsp. softened Cream Cheese
- 1/2 tsp. Pumpkin Spice
- 1/2 tsp. Baking Powder
- 1/2 tsp. Vanilla
- 1 tsp. Choczero Maple Syrup or 1/8 tsp. Maple Extract

Filling:
- 2 tbsp. Cream Cheese
- 1 tbsp. Lakanto Powdered Sweetener
- 1/4 tsp. Vanilla Extract

Directions:
1. Heat mini waffle maker.
2. Mix all chaffle ingredients in a shallow mixing bowl.
3. Set half of the chaffle batter into the waffle irons middle. Allow for 3-5 minutes of Cooking time.
4. Remove carefully and repeat with the second chaffle. Set aside to crisp when preparing the filling.
5. Mix all frosting ingredients in a mixing bowl with a whisk or fork. Between the two chaffles, spread frosting. Have fun!
6. Optional toppings include whipped cream, crushed pecans, and Choczero maple syrup.

Nutrition: Calories: 231 Carbohydrate: 2g Fat: 18g Protein: 13g

Pumpkin Spice Chaffles

Preparation Time: 2 minutes
Cooking Time: 12 minutes
Servings: 3

Ingredients:
- 1 cup of mozzarella cheese
- 2 tbsp. almond flour
- 1 tsp. baking powder
- 2 eggs
- 1/2 tsp. pumpkin pie spice
- 2 tsp. of Swerve

Directions:
1. Mix the eggs, almond flour, mozzarella cheese, baking powder, pumpkin pie spice, and swerve in a shallow mixing bowl.
2. Pour the mixture into a small food processor and heat until smooth.
3. Cooking for 3-4 minutes with 1/3 of the batter in your mini waffle maker. Cooking the remaining batter to produce a second chaffle, and then repeat until all of the pumpkin spice chaffles have been made.
4. Serve with a drizzle of swerve confectioners sweetener or low carb syrup and butter.

Nutrition: Calories 90 Fats 3.32g Carbs 2.97g Net carbs 2.17g Protein 12.09g

Simple Blueberry Chaffle

Preparation Time: 7 minutes
Cooking Time: 3 minutes
Servings: 2

Ingredients:

- 1 Egg (beaten)
- 1/2 cup of Mozzarella cheese (grated)
- 1 tsp. Erythritol
- 1/2 tsp. Baking powder
- 1 tsp. Blueberry extract
- 1/2 tsp. Cinnamon
- 12 Blueberries (fresh)

Directions:

1. Heat the mini-waffle maker with Cooking spray before ready to use.
2. Mix the entire ingredient*s in a bowl (except the blueberries). You should also use a mixer to mix the ingredients.
3. Pour ample batter into the waffle maker's middle and fan it out to the corners. If you overfill the first one, fill it up a little less every time to prevent spilling. 6 new blueberries on top
4. Allow 3 1/2 minutes to Cooking with the lid closed.
5. Remove the chaffle and set it aside to cool for 5 minutes on a cooling rack; repeat for the second chaffle. Add a dollop of whipped cream and a couple new blueberries on top.

Nutrition: Calories: 121 Carbohydrates: 3g Protein: 9g Fat: 8g Cholesterol: 104mg Sodium: 208mg

Sweet Keto Chaffles

Preparation Time: 7 minutes
Cooking Time: 10 minutes
Servings: 2

Ingredients:
- 1 large egg
- 1/2 cup of shredded low moisture mozzarella
- 1/4 cup of almond flour
- 1/8 tsp. of gluten-free baking powder
- 3 tbsp. of granulated low-carb sweetener such as Erythritol or Swerve or brown sugar substitute

Directions:
1. To make the waffles, measure out all of the ingredients. Using a standard waffle maker to preheat a mini waffle maker.
2. You may either mix all of the ingredients together in a bowl or blend them together. In a mixer or food processor, mix the egg, mozzarella, almond flour, and baking powder.
3. After that, stir in the sweetener. The dough would be a bit runnier if the sweetener is added before mixing, so I like to add mine after.
4. Spoon one-third of the batter (3 to 4 tsp., around 55 g/1.9 oz.) into the hot waffle maker to produce three tiny waffles.
5. Cooking for 3 to 4 minutes with the waffle maker closed.
6. When you're done, remove the lid and set it aside to cool for a few moments. Transfer the chaffle to a cooling rack softly with a spatula. Continue for the remaining hitter.
7. Allow the chaffles to cool fully before serving. When they're hot, they'll be fluffy, but when they cool, they'll crisp up. Top with full-fat milk, coconut yogurt, whipped cream, bananas, and/or bacon syrup for a low-carb dessert. Serve with One-Minute Chocolate Milk, hot or cold!
8. Enjoy right away, or keep the chaffles in a sealed jar at room temperature for up to 3 days, or in the fridge for up to a week, without any toppings. The jar will hold them fluffy, but if you like them crispy, you can leave them out.

Nutrition: Protein: 45 Fat: 47 Carbohydrates: 8

Open-Faced Grilled Ham and Cheese Sandwich

Preparation Time: 10 minutes
Cooking Time: 15 minutes
Servings: 1

Ingredients:
- Olive oil
- 4 slices white toasted sandwich bread
- 1 tbsp. mustard
- 4 slices Applegate Naturals Slow cooked Ham
- 4 slices Applegate Organics American Cheese
- 2 thickly sliced tomatoes
- 1 thinly sliced red onion
- Salt and freshly ground black pepper
- Finely chopped chives, for garnish

Directions:
1. Heat the oven to 400F. Using olive oil, coat a small sheet pan.
2. Arrange the toast slices on the plate. Cover every slice of toast with 1 slice of ham, 1 slice of cheese, 2 slices of tomato, and a few slices of red onion, and spread the mustard on top.
3. Drizzle olive oil over every sandwich and season lightly with salt and pepper.
4. Bake for 10-12 minutes, or until the cheese is bubbling and melted. Serve immediately with chives as a garnish.

Nutrition: Calories: 147 Net Carb: 2.2g Fat: 13g Saturated Fat: 10.7g

Cheesy Chaffle Sandwiches with Avocado and Bacon

Preparation Time: 10 minutes
Cooking Time: 25 minutes
Servings: 8

Ingredients:
- 10 large eggs
- 11/4 cups of shredded sharp Cheddar cheese
- 2 slices center-cut bacon, cooked and crumbled
- 1/2 tsp. ground pepper
- 2 small sliced avocados
- 2 small sliced tomatoes
- 4 large leaves butter head lettuce

Directions:
1. In a bowl, whisk the egg*s until creamy. Add the cheese, crumbled bacon, and pepper as need.
2. Cover a 7-inch round waffle iron (not Belgian) with Cooking spray and preheat it. 2/3 cup of the egg mixture should be poured onto the molten waffle iron. Cooking for 4 to 5 minutes, or until the eggs are set and light golden brown. Go on for the remainder of the egg mixture and Cooking oil in the same manner (making 4 chaffles total).
3. Every chaffle should be quartered. Half of the quarters can be covered in avocado slices, tomato slices, and lettuce slices. Add the remaining chaffle quarters on to. Serve right away.

Nutrition: Carbs 8 g Fat 11 g Protein 5 g Calories 168

SIMPLE CHAFFLE

Layered Cheese Chaffles

Preparation time: 8 minutes
Cooking Time: 5 Minutes
Servings: 2

Ingredients:
- 1 organic egg, beaten
- 1/3 cup Cheddar cheese, shredded
- 1/2 teaspoon ground flaxseed
- 1/4 teaspoon organic baking powder
- 2 tablespoons Parmesan cheese, shredded

Directions:
1. Preheat a mini waffle iron and then grease it.
2. In a bowl, et all the ingredients except Parmesan and beat until well combined.
3. Place half the Parmesan cheese in the bottom of preheated waffle iron.
4. Place half of the egg mixture over cheese and top with the remaining Parmesan cheese.
5. Cooking for about 3-minutes or until golden brown.
6. Serve warm.

Nutrition: Calories: 264 Net Carb: 1. Fat: 20g Saturated Fat: 11.1g Carbohydrates: 2

Chaffles with Keto Ice Cream

Preparation time: 10 minutes
Cooking Time: 14 Minutes
Servings: 2

Ingredients:

- 1 egg, beaten
- 1/2 cup finely grated mozzarella cheese
- 1/4 cup almond flour
- 2 tbsp. swerve confectioner's sugar
- 1/8 tsp. xanthan gum
- Low-carb ice cream (flavor of your choice) for serving

Directions:

1. Preheat the waffle iron.
2. In a medium bowl, merge all the ingredients except the ice cream.
3. Open the iron and add half of the mixture. Close and Cooking until crispy, 7 minutes.
4. Transfer the chaffle to a plate and make second one with the remaining batter.
5. On each chaffle, add a scoop of low carb ice cream, fold into half-moons and enjoy.

Nutrition: Calories 89 Fats 48g Carbs 1.67g Net Carbs 1.37g Protein 5.91g

Vanilla Mozzarella Chaffles

Preparation time: 10 minutes
Cooking Time: 12 Minutes
Servings: 2

Ingredients:
- 1 organic egg, beaten
- 1 teaspoon organic vanilla extract
- 1 tablespoon almond flour
- 1 teaspoon organic baking powder
- Pinch of ground cinnamon
- 1 cup Mozzarella cheese, shredded

Directions:
1. Preheat a mini waffle iron and then grease it.
2. In a bowl, place the egg and vanilla extract and beat until well combined.
3. Add the flour, baking powder and cinnamon and mix well.
4. Add the Mozzarella cheese and stir to combine.
5. In a small bowl, place the egg and Mozzarella cheese and stir to combine.
6. Set half of the mixture into preheated waffle iron and Cooking for about 5-minutes or until golden brown.
7. Repeat with the remaining mixture.
8. Serve warm.

Nutrition: Calories: 103 Net Carb: 2.4g Fat: 6.6g Saturated Fat: 2.3g Carbohydrates: 2.

Egg-free Psyllium Husk Chaffles

Preparation time: 8 minutes
Cooking Time: 4 Minutes
Servings: 3

Ingredients:
- 1 ounce Mozzarella cheese, shredded
- 1 tablespoon cream cheese, softened
- 1 tablespoon psyllium husk powder

Directions:
1. Preheat a waffle iron and then grease it.
2. In a blender, place all ingredients and pulse until a slightly crumbly mixture forms.
3. Place the mixture into preheated waffle iron and Cooking for about 4 minutes or until golden brown.
4. Serve warm.

Nutrition: Calories: 137 Net Carb: 1.3g Fat: 8.8g Saturated Fat: 2g Carbohydrates: 1.3g Sugar: 0g Protein: 9.5g

Cheddar and Egg White Chaffles

Preparation time: 9 minutes
Cooking Time: 12 Minutes
Servings: 2

Ingredients:
- 2 egg whites
- 1 cup Cheddar cheese, shredded

Directions:
1. Preheat a mini waffle iron and then grease it.
2. In a small bowl, set the egg whites and cheese and stir to combine.
3. Place 1/4 of the mixture into preheated waffle iron and Cooking for about 4 minutes or until golden brown.
4. Repeat with the remaining mixture.
5. Serve warm.

Nutrition: Calories: 122 Net Carb: 0.5g Fat: 9.4g Saturated Fat: Carbohydrates: 0.5g Sugar: 0.3g Protein: 8.8g

Spicy Shrimp and Chaffles

Preparation time: 9 minutes
Cooking Time: 31 Minutes
Servings: 4

Ingredients:

For the shrimp:
- 1 tbsp. olive oil
- 1 lb. jumbo shrimp, peeled and deveined
- 1 tbsp. Creole seasoning
- Salt to taste
- 2 tbsp. hot sauce
- 3 tbsp. butter
- 2 tbsp. chopped fresh scallions to garnish

For the chaffles:
- 2 eggs, beaten
- 1 cup finely grated Monterey Jack cheese

Directions:

For the shrimp:
1. Set the olive oil in a medium skillet over medium heat.
2. Season the shrimp with the Creole seasoning and salt. Cooking in the oil until pink and opaque on both sides, 2 minutes.
3. Pour in the hot sauce and butter. Mix well until the shrimp is adequately coated in the sauce, 1 minute.
4. Turn the heat off and set aside.

For the chaffles:
1. Preheat the waffle iron.
2. In a medium bowl, merge the eggs and Monterey Jack cheese.
3. Open the iron and add a quarter of the mixture. Close and Cooking until crispy, 7 minutes.
4. Transfer the chaffle to a plate and make 3 more chaffles in the same manner.
5. Cut the chaffles into quarters and place on a plate.
6. Set with the shrimp and garnish with the scallions.
7. Serve warm.

Nutrition: Calories 342 Fats 19.75g Carbs 2.8g Net Carbs 2.3g Protein 36.01g

Creamy Chicken Chaffle Sandwich

Preparation time: 10 minutes
Cooking Time: 10 Minutes
Servings: 2

Ingredients:
- Cooking spray
- 1 cup chicken breast fillet, cubed
- Salt and pepper to taste
- 1/4 cup all-purpose cream
- 4 garlic chaffles
- Parsley, chopped

Directions:
1. Spray your pan with oil.
2. Put it over medium heat.
3. Add the chicken fillet cubes.
4. Season with salt and pepper.
5. Reduce heat and add the cream.
6. Spread chicken mixture on top of the chaffle.
7. Garnish with parsley and top with another chaffle.

Nutrition: Calories 273 Total Fat 34g Saturated Fat 4.1g Cholesterol 62mg Sodium 373mg Total Carbohydrate 22.5g Protein 17.5g Potassium 177mg

Chaffle Cannoli

Preparation time: 9 minutes
Cooking Time: 28 Minutes
Servings: 2

Ingredients:

For the chaffles:
- 1 large egg
- 1 egg yolk
- 3 tbsp. butter, melted
- 1 tbsp. swerve confectioner's
- 1 cup finely grated Parmesan cheese
- 2 tbsp. finely grated mozzarella cheese

For the cannoli filling:
- 1/2 cup ricotta cheese
- 2 tbsp. swerve confectioner's sugar
- 1 tsp. vanilla extract
- 2 tbsp. unsweetened chocolate chips for garnishing

Directions:
1. Preheat the waffle iron.
2. Meanwhile, in a medium bowl, merge all the ingredients for the chaffles.
3. Open the iron; pour in a quarter of the mixture, cover, and Cooking until crispy, 7 minutes.
4. Remove the chaffle onto a plate and make 3 more with the remaining batter.
5. Meanwhile, for the cannoli filling:
6. Beat the ricotta cheese and swerve confectioner's sugar until smooth. Mix in the vanilla.
7. On each chaffle, spread some of the filling and wrap over.
8. Garnish the creamy ends with some chocolate chips.
9. Serve immediately.

Nutrition: Calories 308 Fats 25.05g Carbs 5.17g Net Carbs 5.17g Protein 15.18g

VEGETARIAN

Crispy Bagel Chaffles

Preparation time: 5 minutes
Cooking Time: 30 Minutes
Servings: 2

Ingredients:
- 2 eggs
- 1/2 cup parmesan cheese
- 1 tsp. bagel seasoning
- 1/2 cup mozzarella cheese
- 2 teaspoons almond flour

Directions:
1. Turn on waffle maker to heat and oil it with Cooking spray.
2. Evenly sprinkle half of cheeses to a griddle and let them melt. Then toast for 30 seconds and leave them wait for batter.
3. Whisk eggs, other half of cheeses, almond flour, and bagel seasoning in a small bowl.
4. Pour batter into the waffle maker. Cooking for minutes.
5. Let cool for 2-3 minutes before serving.

Nutrition: Calories 117 Fat 2.1g Carbs 18.2g, Protein 22.7g

Broccoli and Almond Flour Chaffles

Preparation time: 6 minutes
Cooking Time: 8 Minutes
Servings: 2

Ingredients:
- 1 organic egg, beaten
- 1/2 cup Cheddar cheese, shredded
- 1/4 cup fresh broccoli, chopped
- 1 tablespoon almond flour
- 1/4 teaspoon garlic powder

Directions:
1. Preheat a mini waffle iron and then grease it.
2. In a bowl, place all ingredients and mix until well merged.
3. Set half of the mixture into preheated waffle iron and Cooking for about 4 minutes or until golden brown.
4. Repeat with the remaining mixture.
5. Serve warm.

Nutrition: Calories 221 Protein 17 g Carbs 31 g Fat 8 g

Cheddar Jalapeño Chaffle

Preparation time: 6 minutes
Cooking Time: 5 Minutes
Servings: 2

Ingredients:
- 2 large eggs
- 1/2 cup shredded mozzarella
- 1/4 cup almond flour
- 1/2 tsp. baking powder
- 1/4 cup shredded cheddar cheese
- 2 Tbsp. diced jalapeños jarred or canned

For the toppings:
- 1/2 Cooked bacon, chopped
- 2 Tbsp. cream cheese
- 1/4 jalapeño slices

Directions:
1. Turn on waffle maker to heat and oil it with Cooking spray.
2. Mix mozzarella, eggs, baking powder, almond flour, and garlic powder in a bowl.
3. Sprinkle 2 Tbsp. cheddar cheese in a thin layer on waffle maker, and 1/2 jalapeño.
4. Ladle half of the egg mixture on top of the cheese and jalapeños.
5. Cooking for minutes, or until done.
6. Repeat for the second chaffle.
7. Top with cream cheese, bacon, and jalapeño slices.

Nutrition: Calories 221 Protein 13 g Carbs 1 g Fat 34 g Sodium 80 mg

Rosemary in Chaffles

Preparation time: 6 minutes
Cooking Time: 8 Minutes
Servings: 2

Ingredients:
- 1 organic egg, beaten
- 1/2 cup Cheddar cheese, shredded
- 1 tablespoon almond flour
- 1 tablespoon fresh rosemary, chopped
- salt and ground black pepper

Directions:
1. Preheat a mini waffle iron and then grease it.
2. For chaffles: In a medium bowl, place all ingredients and with a fork, mix until well merged.
3. Set half of the mixture into preheated waffle iron and Cooking for about 4 minutes or until golden brown.
4. Repeat with the remaining mixture.
5. Serve warm.

Nutrition: Calories 221 Protein 12 g Carbs 29 g, Fat 8 g Sodium 398 mg

Zucchini in Chaffles

Preparation time: 10 minutes
Cooking Time: 18 Minutes
Servings: 2

Ingredients:

- 2 large zucchinis, grated and squeezed
- 2 large organic eggs
- 2/3 cup Cheddar cheese, shredded
- 2 tablespoons coconut flour
- 1/2 teaspoon garlic powder
- 1/2 teaspoon red pepper flakes, crushed
- Salt, to taste

Directions:

1. Preheat a waffle iron and then grease it.
2. In a medium bowl, set all ingredients and, mix until well combined.
3. Place 1/4 of the mixture into preheated waffle iron and Cooking for about 4-41/2 minutes or until golden brown.
4. Repeat with the remaining mixture.
5. Serve warm.

Nutrition: Calories 311 Protein 16 g Carbs 17 g Fat 15 g

Garlic and Onion Powder Chaffles

Preparation time: 5 minutes
Cooking Time: 5 Minutes
Servings: 2

Ingredients:
- 1 organic egg, beaten
- 1/4 cup Cheddar cheese, shredded
- 2 tablespoons almond flour
- 1/2 teaspoon organic baking powder
- 1/4 teaspoon garlic powder
- 1/4 teaspoon onion powder
- Pinch of salt

Directions:
1. Preheat a waffle iron and then grease it.
2. In a bowl, set all the ingredients and beat until well combined.
3. Place the mixture into preheated waffle iron and Cooking for about 5 minutes or until golden brown.
4. Serve warm.

Nutrition: Calories 249, Protein 12 g Carbs 30 g Fat 10 g

Savory Bagel Seasoning Chaffles

Preparation time: 10 minutes
Cooking Time: 5 Minutes
Servings: 4

Ingredients:
- 2 tbsps. everything bagel seasoning
- 2 eggs
- 1 cup mozzarella cheese
- 1/2 cup grated parmesan

Directions:
1. Preheat the square waffle maker and grease with Cooking spray.
2. Mix together eggs, mozzarella cheese and grated cheese in a bowl.
3. Set half of the batter in the waffle maker.
4. Sprinkle 1 tbsp. of the everything bagel seasoning over batter.
5. Close the lid.
6. Cooking chaffles for about 3-4 minutes Utes.
7. Repeat with the remaining batter.
8. Serve hot and enjoy!

Nutrition: Calories 64 Fat 3.1 Fiber 3 Carbs 7.1 Protein 2.8

Dried Herbs Chaffle

Preparation time: 6 minutes
Cooking Time: 8 Minutes
Servings: 2

Ingredients:
- 1 organic egg, beaten
- 1/2 cup Cheddar cheese, shredded
- 1 tablespoon almond flour
- Pinch of dried thyme, crushed
- Pinch of dried rosemary, crushed

Directions:
1. Preheat a mini waffle iron and then grease it.
2. In a bowl, place all the ingredients and beat until well merged.
3. Set half of the mixture into preheated waffle iron and Cooking for about 4 minutes or until golden brown.
4. Repeat with the remaining mixture.
5. Serve warm.

Nutrition: Calories 80 Fat 2.5 Fiber 3.9 Carbs 10.9 Protein 4

Zucchini and Basil Chaffles

Preparation time: 6 minutes
Cooking Time: 10 Minutes
Servings: 2

Ingredients:

- 1 organic egg, beaten
- 1/4 cup Mozzarella cheese, shredded
- 2 tablespoons Parmesan cheese, grated
- 1/2 of small zucchini, grated and squeezed
- 1/4 teaspoon dried basil, crushed
- Freshly ground black pepper, as required

Directions:

1. Preheat a mini waffle iron and then grease it.
2. In a medium bowl, set all ingredients and mix until well combined.
3. Set half of the mixture into preheated waffle iron and Cooking for about 4-5 minutes or until golden brown.
4. Repeat with the remaining mixture.
5. Serve warm.

Nutrition: Calories 43 Fat 3.4 Carbs 3.4 Protein 1.3

Turkey Chaffle Sandwich

Preparation Time: 5 minutes
Cooking Time: 15 minutes
Serving: 4

Ingredients:
Batter

- 4 eggs
- 1/4 cup cream cheese
- 1 cup grated mozzarella cheese
- Salt and pepper to taste
- 1 teaspoon dried dill
- 1/2 teaspoon onion powder
- 1/2 teaspoon garlic powder
- Juicy chicken
- 2 tablespoons butter
- 1 pound chicken breast
- Salt and pepper to taste
- 1 teaspoon dried dill
- 2 tablespoons heavy cream

Other

- 2 tablespoons butter to brush the waffle maker
- 4 lettuce leaves to garnish the sandwich
- 4 tomato slices to garnish the sandwich

Directions

1. Preheat the waffle maker.
2. Add the eggs, cream cheese, mozzarella cheese, salt and pepper, dried dill, onion powder and garlic powder to a bowl.
3. Mix everything with a fork just until batter forms.
4. Brush the heated waffle maker with butter and add a few tablespoons of the batter.
5. Close the lid and Cooking for about 5–7 minutes depending on your waffle maker.
6. Meanwhile, heat some butter in a nonstick pan.
7. Season the chicken with salt and pepper and sprinkle with dried dill. Pour the heavy cream on top.
8. Cooking the chicken slices for about 10 minutes or until golden brown.
9. Cut each chaffle in half.
10. On one half add a lettuce leaf, tomato slice, and chicken slice. Cover with the other chaffle half to make a sandwich.
11. Serve and enjoy.

Nutrition Calories 381 Fat 26.3 g Carbs 2.5 g Sugar 1 g, Protein 32.9 g Sodium 278 Mg

Mozzarella Chicken Jalapeno Chaffle

Preparation Time: 5 minutes
Cooking Time: 8 minutes
Serving: 2

Ingredients:
Batter

- 1/2 pound ground chicken
- 4 eggs
- 1 cup grated mozzarella cheese
- 2 tablespoons sour cream
- 1 green jalapeno, chopped
- Salt and pepper to taste
- 1 teaspoon dried oregano
- 1/2 teaspoon dried garlic

Other

- 2 tablespoons butter to brush the waffle maker
- 1/4 cup sour cream to garnish
- 1 green jalapeno, diced, to garnish

Directions

1. Preheat the waffle maker.
2. Add the ground chicken, eggs, mozzarella cheese, sour cream, chopped jalapeno, salt and pepper, dried oregano and dried garlic to a bowl.
3. Mix everything until batter forms.
4. Brush the heated waffle maker with butter and add a few tablespoons of the batter.
5. Close the lid and Cooking for about 8–10 minutes depending on your waffle maker.
6. Serve with a tablespoon of sour cream and sliced jalapeno on top.

Nutrition Calories 284 Fat 19.4 G Carbs 2.2 G Sugar 0.6 G, Protein 24.7 G Sodium 204 Mg

Turkey BBQ Sauce Chaffle

Preparation Time: 5 minutes
Cooking Time: 10 minutes
Serving: 4

Ingredients:
Batter

- 1/2 pound ground turkey meat
- 3 eggs
- 1 cup grated Swiss cheese
- 1/4 cup cream cheese
- 1/4 cup BBQ sauce
- 1 teaspoon dried oregano
- Salt and pepper to taste
- 2 cloves garlic, minced

Other

- 2 tablespoons butter to brush the waffle maker
- 1/4 cup BBQ sauce for serving
- 2 tablespoons freshly chopped parsley for garnish

Directions

1. Preheat the waffle maker.
2. Add the ground turkey, eggs, grated Swiss cheese, cream cheese, BBQ sauce, dried oregano, salt and pepper, and minced garlic to a bowl.
3. Mix everything until combined and batter forms.
4. Brush the heated waffle maker with butter and add a few tablespoons of the batter.
5. Close the lid and Cooking for about 8–10 minutes depending on your waffle maker.
6. Serve each chaffle with a tablespoon of BBQ sauce and a sprinkle of freshly chopped parsley.

Nutrition Calories 365 Fat 23.7 g Carbs 13.7 g Sugar 8.8 g, Protein 23.5 g Sodium 595 mg Protein 27.4 g Sodium 291 Mg

Beef and Sour Cream Chaffle

Preparation Time: 5 minutes
Cooking Time: 20 minutes
Serving: 4

Ingredients:
Batter
- 4 eggs
- 2 cups grated mozzarella cheese
- 3 tablespoons coconut flour
- 3 tablespoons almond flour
- 2 teaspoons baking powder
- Salt and pepper to taste
- 1 tablespoon freshly chopped parsley
- Seasoned beef
- 1 pound beef tenderloin
- Salt and pepper to taste
- 2 tablespoons olive oil
- 1 tablespoon Dijon mustard

Other
- 2 tablespoons olive oil to brush the waffle maker
- 1/4 cup sour cream for garnish
- 2 tablespoons freshly chopped spring onion for garnish

Directions
1. Preheat the waffle maker.
2. Add the eggs, grated mozzarella cheese, coconut flour, almond flour, baking powder, salt and pepper and freshly chopped parsley to a bowl.
3. Mix until just combined and batter forms.
4. Brush the heated waffle maker with olive oil and add a few tablespoons of the batter.
5. Close the lid and Cooking for about 5–7 minutes depending on your waffle maker.
6. Meanwhile, heat the olive oil in a nonstick pan over medium heat.
7. Season the beef tenderloin with salt and pepper and spread the whole piece of beef tenderloin with Dijon mustard.
8. Cooking on each side for about 4–5 minutes.
9. Serve each chaffle with sour cream and slices of the cooked beef tenderloin.
10. Garnish with freshly chopped spring onion.
11. Serve and enjoy.

Nutrition Calories 543 Fat 37 g Carbs 7.9 g Sugar 0.5 g   Protein 44.9 g Sodium 269 Mg

Beef Chaffle Sandwich Recipe

Preparation Time: 5 minutes
Cooking Time: 15 minutes
Serving: 4

Ingredients:
Batter

- 3 eggs
- 2 cups grated mozzarella cheese
- 1/4 cup cream cheese
- Salt and pepper to taste
- 1 teaspoon Italian seasoning

Beef

- 2 tablespoons butter
- 1 pound beef tenderloin
- Salt and pepper to taste
- 2 teaspoons Dijon mustard
- 1 teaspoon dried paprika

Other

- 2 tablespoons Cooking spray to brush the waffle maker
- 4 lettuce leaves for serving
- 4 tomato slices for serving
- 4 leaves fresh basil

Directions

1. Preheat the waffle maker.
2. Add the eggs, grated mozzarella cheese, salt and pepper and Italian seasoning to a bowl.
3. Mix until combined and batter forms.
4. Brush the heated waffle maker with Cooking spray and add a few tablespoons of the batter.
5. Close the lid and Cooking for about 5–7 minutes depending on your waffle maker.
6. Meanwhile, melt and heat the butter in a nonstick frying pan.
7. Season the beef loin with salt and pepper, brush it with Dijon mustard, and sprinkle some dried paprika on top.
8. Cooking the beef on each side for about 5 minutes.
9. Thinly slice the beef and assemble the chaffle sandwiches.
10. Cut each chaffle in half and on one half place a lettuce leaf, tomato slice, basil leaf, and some sliced beef.
11. Cover with the other chaffle half and serve.

Nutrition Calories 477 Fat 32.8g Carbs 2.3 g Sugar 0.9 g, Protein 42.2 g Sodium 299 Mg

Beef Meatballs on a Chaffle

Preparation Time: 5 minutes
Cooking Time: 20 minutes
Serving: 4

Ingredients:
Batter

- 4 eggs
- 2 1/2 cups grated gouda cheese
- 1/4 cup heavy cream
- Salt and pepper to taste
- 1 spring onion, finely chopped

Beef meatballs

- 1 pound ground beef
- Salt and pepper to taste
- 2 teaspoons Dijon mustard
- 1 spring onion, finely chopped
- 5 tablespoons almond flour
- 2 tablespoons butter

Other

- 2 tablespoons Cooking spray to brush the waffle maker
- 2 tablespoons freshly chopped parsley

Directions
1. Preheat the waffle maker.
2. Add the eggs, grated gouda cheese, heavy cream, salt and pepper and finely chopped spring onion to a bowl.
3. Mix until combined and batter forms.
4. Brush the heated waffle maker with Cooking spray and add a few tablespoons of the batter.
5. Close the lid and Cooking for about 5–7 minutes depending on your waffle maker.
6. Meanwhile, mix the ground beef meat, salt and pepper, Dijon mustard, chopped spring onion and almond flour in a large bowl.
7. Form small meatballs with your hands.
8. Warmth the butter in a nonstick frying pan and Cooking the beef meatballs for about 3–4 minutes on each side.
9. Serve each chaffle with a couple of meatballs and some freshly chopped parsley on top.

Nutrition Calories 670 Fat 47.4g Carbs 4.6 g Sugar 1.7 g,   Protein 54.9 g Sodium 622 Mg

Beef Chaffle Taco

Preparation Time: 5 minutes
Cooking Time: 15 minutes
Serving: 4

Ingredients:
Batter

- 4 eggs
- 2 cups grated cheddar cheese
- 1/4 cup heavy cream
- Salt and pepper to taste
- 1/4 cup almond flour
- 2 teaspoons baking powder

Beef

- 2 tablespoons butter
- 1/2 onion, diced
- 1 pound ground beef
- Salt and pepper to taste
- 1 teaspoon dried oregano
- 1 tablespoon sugar-free ketchup

Other

- 2 tablespoons Cooking spray to brush the waffle maker
- 2 tablespoons freshly chopped parsley

Directions

1. Preheat the waffle maker.
2. Add the eggs, grated cheddar cheese, heavy cream, salt and pepper, almond flour and baking powder to a bowl.
3. Brush the heated waffle maker with Cooking spray and add a few tablespoons of the batter.
4. Close the lid and Cooking for about 5–7 minutes depending on your waffle maker.
5. Once the chaffle is ready, place it in a napkin holder to harden into the shape of a taco as it cools.
6. Meanwhile, melt and heat the butter in a nonstick frying pan and start Cooking the diced onion.
7. Once the onion is tender, add the ground beef. Season with salt and pepper and dried oregano and stir in the sugar-free ketchup.
8. Cooking for about 7 minutes.
9. Serve the Cooked ground meat in each taco chaffle sprinkled with some freshly chopped parsley.

Nutrition Calories 719 Fat 51.7 g Carbs 7.3 g Sugar 1.3 g, Protein 56.1 g Sodium 573 Mg

Beef Meatza Chaffle

Preparation Time: 5 minutes
Cooking Time: 20 minutes
Serving: 4

Ingredients:
- Meatza chaffle batter
- 1/2-pound ground beef
- 4 eggs
- 2 cups grated cheddar cheese
- Salt and pepper to taste
- 1 teaspoon Italian seasoning
- 2 tablespoons tomato sauce

Other
- 2 tablespoons Cooking spray to brush the waffle maker
- 1/4 cup tomato sauce for serving
- 2 tablespoons freshly chopped basil for serving

Directions
1. Preheat the waffle maker.
2. Add the ground beef, eggs, grated cheddar cheese, salt and pepper, Italian seasoning and tomato sauce to a bowl.
3. Mix until everything is fully combined.
4. Brush the heated waffle maker with Cooking spray and add a few tablespoons of the batter.
5. Close the lid and Cooking for about 7–10 minutes depending on your waffle maker.
6. Serve with tomato sauce and freshly chopped basil on top.

Nutrition Calories 470 Fat 34.6 g Carbs 2.5 g Sugar 1.7 g, Protein 36.5 Sodium 581 Mg

CAKE AND SANDWICH

Pecan Pie Cake Chaffle

Preparation Time: 15 minutes
Cooking Time: 25 minutes
Servings: 2

Ingredients:
For Pecan Pie Chaffle:
- Egg: 1
- Cream cheese: 2 tbsp.
- Maple extract: 1/2 tbsp.
- Almond flour: 4 tbsp.
- Serkin Gold: 1 tbsp.
- Baking powder: 1/2 tbsp.
- Pecan: 2 tbsp. chopped
- Heavy whipping cream: 1 tbsp.

For Pecan Pie Filling:
- Butter: 2 tbsp.
- Serkin Gold: 1 tbsp.
- Pecan: 2 tbsp. chopped
- Heavy whipping cream: 2 tbsp.
- Maple syrup: 2 tbsp.
- Egg yolk: 2 large
- Salt: a pinch

Directions:
1. In a small saucepan, add sweetener, butter, syrups, and heavy whipping cream and use a low flame to heat
2. Mix all the ingredients well together
3. Remove from heat and add egg yolks and mix
4. Now put it on heat again and stir
5. Add pecan and salt to the mixture and let it simmer
6. It will thicken then detach from heat and let it rest
7. For the chaffles, add all the ingredients except pecans and blend
8. Now add pecan with a spoon
9. Preheat a mini waffle maker if needed and grease it
10. Pour the mixture to the lower plate of the waffle maker and spread it evenly to cover the plate properly and close the lid
11. Cooking for at least 4 minutes to get the desired crunch
12. Remove the chaffle from the heat and keep aside for around one minute
13. Make as many chaffles as your mixture and waffle maker allow
14. Add 1/3 the previously prepare pecan pie filling to the chaffle and arrange like a cake

Nutrition: Calories 141 Protein 10 g Carbohydrates 15 g Fat 0 g Sodium 113 mg

German Chocolate Chaffle Cake

Preparation Time: 5 minutes
Cooking Time: 10 minutes
Servings: 2

Ingredients:
For Chocolate Chaffle:

- Egg: 1
- Cream cheese: 2 tbsp.
- Powdered sweetener: 1 tbsp.
- Vanilla extract: 1/2 tbsp.
- Instant coffee powder: 1/4 tsp.
- Almond flour: 1 tbsp.
- Cocoa powder: 1 tbsp. (unsweetened)

For Filling:

- Egg Yolk: 1
- Heavy cream: 1/4 cup
- Butter: 1 tbsp.
- Powdered sweetener: 2 tbsp.
- Caramel: 1/2 tsp.
- Coconut flakes: 1/4 cup
- Coconut flour: 1 tsp.
- Pecans: 1/4 cups chopped

Directions:

1. Preheat a mini waffle maker if needed and grease it
2. In a mixing bowl, beat eggs and add the remaining chaffle ingredients
3. Mix them all well
4. Pour the mixture to the lower plate of the waffle maker and spread it evenly to cover the plate properly and close the lid
5. Cooking for at least 4 minutes to get the desired crunch
6. Remove the chaffle from the heat and let them cool completely
7. Make as many chaffles as your mixture and waffle maker allow
8. In a small pan, mix heavy cream, egg yolk, sweetener, and butter at low heat for around 5 minutes
9. Remove from heat and add the remaining ingredients to make the filling
10. Stack chaffles on one another and add filling in between to enjoy the cake

Nutrition: Calories 147 Fat 11.5 g Protein 9.8 g

Almond Chocolate Chaffle Cake

Preparation Time: 5 minutes
Cooking Time: 10 minutes
Servings: 2

Ingredients:
For Chocolate Chaffle:
Egg: 1

- Cream cheese: 2 tbsp.
- Powdered sweetener: 1 tbsp.
- Vanilla extract: 1/2 tbsp.
- Instant coffee powder: 1/4 tsp.
- Almond flour: 1 tbsp.
- Cocoa powder: 1 tbsp. (unsweetened)

For Coconut Filling:
- Melted Coconut Oil: 1 1/2 tbsp.
- Heavy cream: 1 tbsp.
- Cream cheese: 4 tbsp.
- Powdered sweetener: 1 tbsp.
- Vanilla extract: 1/2 tbsp.
- Coconut: 1/4 cup finely shredded
- Whole almonds: 14

Directions:
1. Preheat a mini waffle maker if needed and grease it
2. In a mixing bowl, add all the chaffle ingredients
3. Mix them all well
4. Pour the mixture to the lower plate of the waffle maker and spread it evenly to cover the plate properly
5. Close the lid
6. Cooking for at least 4 minutes to get the desired crunch
7. Remove the chaffle from the heat and keep aside for around one minute
8. Make as many chaffles as your mixture and waffle maker allow
9. Except for almond, add all the filling ingredients in a bowl and mix well
10. Spread the filling on the chaffle and spread almonds on top with another chaffle at almonds stack the chaffles and fillings like a cake and enjoy

Nutrition Calories 238 Fat 18.4g Protein 14.3g

Carrot Cake Chaffle

Preparation Time: 10 minutes
Cooking Time: 15 minutes
Servings: 2

Ingredients:
For Carrot Chaffle Cake:

- Carrot: 1/2 cup (shredded)
- Egg: 1
- Heavy whipping cream: 2 tbsp.
- Butter: 2 tbsp. (melted)
- Powdered sweetener: 2 tbsp.
- Walnuts: 1 tbsp. (chopped)
- Almond flour: 3/4 cup
- Cinnamon powder: 2 tsp.
- Baking powder: 1 tsp.
- Pumpkin sauce: 1 tsp.

For Cream Cheese Frosting:

- Cream cheese: 1/2 cup
- Heavy whipping cream: 2 tbsp.
- Vanilla extract: 1 tsp.
- Powdered sweetener: 1/4 cup

Directions:
1. Merge all the ingredients together one by one until they form a uniform consistency
2. Preheat a mini waffle maker if needed and grease it
3. Pour the mixture to the lower plate of the waffle maker
4. Close the lid
5. Cooking for at least 4 minutes to get the desired crunch
6. Prepare frosting by combining all the ingredients of the cream cheese frosting using a hand mixer
7. Remove the chaffle from the heat and keep aside for around a few minutes
8. Make as many chaffles as your mixture and waffle maker allow
9. Stack the chaffles with frosting in between in such a way that it gives the look of a cake

Nutrition: Calories 555 Total Fat 21.5g Saturated Fat 3.5g Cholesterol 117mg Sodium 654mg

Peanut Butter Keto Chaffle Cake

Preparation Time: 5 minutes
Cooking Time: 10 minutes
Servings: 2

Ingredients:
For Chaffles:

- Egg: 1
- Peanut Butter:: 2 tbsp. (sugar-free)
- Monk fruit: 2 tbsp.
- Baking powder: 1/4 tsp.
- Peanut butter extract: 1/4 tsp.
- Heavy whipping cream: 1 tsp.

For Peanut Butter Frosting:

- Monk fruit: 2 tsp.
- Cream cheese: 2 tbsp.
- Butter: 1 tbsp.
- Peanut butter: 1 tbsp. (sugar-free)
- Vanilla: 1/4 tsp.

Directions:

1. Preheat a mini waffle maker if needed and grease it
2. In a mixing bowl, beat eggs and add all the chaffle ingredients
3. Merge them all well and pour the mixture to the lower plate of the waffle maker
4. Close the lid
5. Cooking for at least 4 minutes to get the desired crunch
6. Remove the chaffle from the heat and keep aside for around a few minutes
7. Make as many chaffles as your mixture and waffle maker allow
8. In a separate bowl, add all the frosting ingredients and whisk well to give it a uniform consistency
9. Assemble chaffles in a way that in between two chaffles you put the frosting and make the cake

Nutrition: Calories: 127 Net Carb: 2gFat: 9g Saturated Fat: 5.3g Carbohydrates: 2.7g Dietary Fiber: 0.7g

Strawberry Shortcake Chaffle

Preparation Time: 5 minutes
Cooking Time: 10 minutes
Servings: 2

Ingredients:
- Egg: 1
- Heavy Whipping Cream: 1 tbsp.
- Any non-sugar sweetener: 2 tbsp.
- Coconut Flour: 1 tsp.
- Cake batter extract: 1/2 tsp.
- Baking powder: 1/4 tsp.
- Strawberry: 4 or as per your taste

Directions:
1. Preheat a mini waffle maker if needed and grease it
2. In a mixing bowl, beat eggs and add non-sugar sweetener, coconut flour, baking powder, and cake batter extract
3. Merge them all well and pour the mixture to the lower plate of the waffle maker
4. Close the lid
5. Cooking for at least 4 minutes to get the desired crunch
6. Remove the chaffle from the heat and keep aside for around two minutes
7. Make as many chaffles as your mixture and waffle maker allow
8. Serve with whipped cream and strawberries on top

Nutrition: Calories 334 Fat 12.1g Protein 48.2g

Italian Cream Chaffle Cake

Preparation Time: 8 minutes
Cooking Time: 12 minutes
Servings: 3

Ingredients:
For Chaffle:

- Egg: 4
- Mozzarella Cheese: 1/2 cup
- Almond flour: 1 tbsp.
- Coconut flour: 4 tbsp.
- Monk fruit sweetener: 1 tbsp.
- Vanilla extract: 1 tsp.
- Baking powder: 1 1/2 tsp.
- Cinnamon powder: 1/2 tsp.
- Butter: 1 tbsp. (melted)
- Coconut: 1 tsp. (shredded)
- Walnuts: 1 tsp. (chopped)
- For Italian Cream Frosting:
- Cream cheese: 4 tbsp.
- Butter: 2 tbsp.
- Vanilla: 1/2 tsp.
- Monk fruit sweetener: 2 tbs.

Directions:

1. Blend eggs, cream cheese, sweetener, vanilla, coconut flour, melted butter, almond flour, and baking powder
2. Make the mixture creamy
3. Preheat a mini waffle maker if needed and grease it
4. Pour the mixture to the lower plate of the waffle maker
5. Close the lid
6. Cooking for at least 4 minutes to get the desired crunch
7. Remove the chaffle from the heat and keep aside to cool it
8. Make as many chaffles as your mixture and waffle maker allow
9. Garnish with shredded coconut and chopped walnuts

Nutrition: Calories: 71 Net Carb: 0.7g Fat: 4.2g Carbohydrates: 0.8g Dietary Fiber: 0.1g

Banana Cake Pudding Chaffle

Preparation Time: 10 minutes
Cooking Time: 1 hour
Servings: 2

Ingredients:
For Banana Chaffle:
- Cream cheese: 2 tbsp.
- Banana extract: 1 tsp.
- Mozzarella cheese: 1/4 cup
- Egg: 1
- Sweetener: 2 tbsp.
- Almond flour: 4 tbsp.
- Baking powder: 1 tsp.

For Banana Pudding:
- Egg yolk: 1 large
- Powdered sweetener: 3 tbsp.
- Xanthan gum: 1/2 tsp.
- Heavy whipping cream: 1/2 cup
- Banana extract: 1/2 tsp.
- Salt: a pinch

Directions:
1. In a pan, add powdered sweetener, heavy cream, and egg yolk and whisk continuously so the mixture thickens
2. Simmer for a minute only
3. Add xanthan gum to the mixture and whisk again
4. Remove the pan from heat and add banana extract and salt and mix them all well
5. Shift the mixture to a glass dish and refrigerate the pudding
6. Preheat a mini waffle maker if needed and grease it
7. In a mixing bowl, add all the chaffle ingredients
8. Merge them all well and pour the mixture to the lower plate of the waffle maker
9. Close the lid
10. Cooking for at least 5 minutes to get the desired crunch
11. Remove the chaffle from the heat and keep aside for around a few minutes
12. Stack chaffles and pudding one by one to form a cake

Nutrition: Calories 156 Protein 14 g, Fat 0 g Cholesterol 0 mg

Cream Coconut Chaffle Cake

Preparation Time: 20 minutes
Cooking Time: 1 hour 20 minutes (depends on your refrigerator)
Servings: 2

Ingredients:
For Chaffles:

- Egg: 2
- Powdered sweetener: 2 tbsp.
- Cream cheese: 2 tbsp.
- Vanilla extract: 1/2 tsp.
- Butter: 1 tbsp. (melted)
- Coconut: 2 tbsp. (shredded)
- Coconut extract: 1/2 tsp.

For Filling:

- Coconut: 1/4 cup (shredded)
- Butter: 2 tsp.
- Monk fruit sweetener: 2 tbsp.
- Xanthan gum: 1/4 tsp.
- Salt: a pinch
- Egg yolks: 2
- Almond: 1/3 cup unsweetened
- Coconut milk: 1/3 cup

For Garnishing:

- Whipped Cream: as per your taste
- Coconut: 1 tbsp. (shredded)

Directions:

1. Preheat a mini waffle maker if needed and grease it
2. In a mixing bowl, add all the chaffle ingredients
3. Merge them all well and pour the mixture to the lower plate of the waffle maker
4. Close the lid
5. Cooking for at least 4 minutes to get the desired crunch
6. Remove the chaffle from the heat and keep aside for around a few minutes
7. Make as many chaffles as your mixture and waffle maker allow
8. For the filling, in a small pan, Cooking almond milk and coconut together on medium heat in such way that it only steams but doesn't boil
9. In another bowl, lightly whish egg yolks and add milk to it continuously
10. Heat the mixture so it thickens, again it must not boil
11. Add sweetener and whisk while adding Xanthan Gum bit by bit
12. Remove from heat and mix all the other ingredients
13. Mix well and refrigerate; the mixture will further thicken when cool
14. Assemble the prepare chaffles and cream on top of one another to make the cake-like shape
15. Garnish with coconuts and whipped cream at the end

Nutrition: Calories: 74 Fat: 2 g Protein: 4 g, Carbohydrates: 10 g Fiber: 0.2 g

CONCLUSION

Getting into ketosis takes around 2-4 days (suggesting carbs are low enough) based on the person. Also, the carb content needed to achieve ketosis can differ between individuals. "Initial weight loss would be very swift but bear in mind that much of it will be contained in glycogen (carbs) and water. Afterward, slow weight loss will follow due to a calorie shortage and consuming more fat as a fuel". As the expression goes, slow and steady wins the race, and this is extremely valid for diets. You will easily lose weight on keto, but you may need to be vigilant with long-term results to help your body adapt to your new diet.

Chaffles can be frozen and processed, so a large proportion can be made and stored for quick and extremely fast meals. If you don't have a waffle maker, just cook the mixture like a pancake in a frying pan, or even cooler, in a fryer-pan. They won't get all the fluffy sides to achieve like you're using a waffle maker, but they're definitely going to taste great. Depending on which cheese you choose, the carbs and net calorie number can shift a little bit. However, in general, whether you use real, whole milk cheese, chaffles are completely carb-free. For up to a month, chaffles will be frozen. However, defrosting them absorbs plenty of moist, which makes it difficult to get their crisp again. Chaffles are rich in fat and moderate in protein and low in carb. Chaffle is a very well established and popular technique to hold people on board. And the chaffles are more durable and better than most forms of keto bread. "What a high-carb diet you may be desirous of. A nonstick waffle maker is something that makes life easier, and it's a trade-off that's happy to embrace for our wellbeing.

The most documented advantage of a keto diet is fast weight reduction. Counter to belief, many people have described becoming less hungry. As well as this, keto can minimize acne, and it may even boost cardiac protection and maintain neural activity, either way, you can contact a medical practitioner to get their opinions and guidelines once you start buying avocado crates and particularly if you have problems with obesity. The requirements of everyone are different and do not fit for you individually what works for the overwhelming majority of citizens. Apart from having an eye on the fat quality, when selecting food products, you can also evaluate the protein. In your keto diet, you just require moderate protein – around 20 percent of your total calorie consumption can come from proteins – and some nuts appear to be rich in protein.

From a mineral and vitamin standpoint, ensure fibrous fruits and vegetables such as cabbage, broccoli and cauliflower are integrated.

Over everything, as for any transition to lifestyle, permit yourself some time to acclimate. You'll see some fast changes almost instantly, but to hold the weight off, you'll have to stay with the plan, even if improvement slows down a little. Slowing down does not mean that the new diet has stopped working; it just means that the body is actually-adjusting itself to meet the new diet. Weight reduction, or something like losing the unnecessary excess weight, is just a side result of a healthy, better lifestyle that can support you in the long run and not only in the short term.

No doubt, chaffles dominated the world of low-carb: they are awesome. For unlimited combinations of seasoning, sweet or savory, you may add and alter using a very simple ingredient with just cheese and eggs. Use it individually or as the resource for seasonings and toppings. A simple calculation of the chaffle is 1/2 cup of 1 egg cheese for every chaffle. Commence adding coconut or almond flour. Check around with the cheeses. Add vegetables, berries, spices or nuts and let the imagination go away.

To sum up, the keto diet is healthy and helpful to your wellbeing and weight reduction if you are very diligent and conscious of it. The best way to monitor your keto commitment is to use a diet tracking app, where you will easily set the target amount of macronutrients / macro breakdown (on keto, it would most definitely be 75 percent fat, 5 percent carbohydrates and 20 percent protein) and check the labels of the food you choose to consume.

Thank you!

CPSIA information can be obtained
at www.ICGtesting.com
Printed in the USA
BVHW022357180521
607645BV00007B/962